Swinging Faster
Lessons on Love, Communication, & Success

Tommy Haydon, Jr.
with **Jessica Hagemann**

CIDER SPOON
STORIES

"*Swinging Faster* is a self-help book for small business owners, employees, couples, and parents--anyone hoping to improve both the personal and professional relationships in their lives."

–Tommy

Cider Spoon Stories
Austin, Texas
www.ciderspoonstories.com

Designed by Cider Spoon Stories
Manufactured in the United States of America

for Reece

Pumpkin picking, Thanksgiving 2013

Acknowledgments

Thank you, Mom and Dad, for your love, your concern, and of course ... for my life.

Thank you, Perry, for always supporting my mother, Suanne, and I.

Thank you, Laura, for your love and loyalty.

Thank you to my "board of directors"--especially you, Myrna--for your tireless ear and impeccable advice.

Thank you, Krista. You are truly one of my favorite people I've ever known.

Thank you to the staff of Tulane Medical Center, Mr. Benson, Ryan, Kai, Ashley, and everyone else to whom I literally owe my continued existence today. I am here because you were there.

Contents

PART THREE: Success

About the Authors

Foreword

This book is divided into three sections: **Love**, **Communication**, and **Success**. Each section offers stories and lessons from my own life re-imagined in the context of relationships in general. Whether you're a business man or woman, a husband or wife, a father or mother ... all of the above ... or prefer to avoid titles entirely ... none of us can deny the power and necessity of relationships, of interacting with others on a daily basis, and of doing so in productive, respectful, and efficient ways.

"Love," "Communication," and "Success" refer to three basic and interchangeable concepts that build on one another over the course of nine chapters. I think you'll find each chapter to be concise, stripped down to the bare essentials, but packed chock-full of accessible lessons applicable to countless real-life scenarios. I suggest you digest no more than one chapter at a sitting, even pausing in the middle to reflect on the occasional provided thought experiment. Your relationships will thank you.

If nothing else, I hope you take away this one simple mantra, and find meaningful ways to embody it starting today:

> Love makes Communication possible.
> Communication breeds Success.

Ready to find out more? Read on.

Yours in the journey,
Tommy Haydon, Jr.

PART ONE
Love

Being deeply loved by someone gives you strength.
Loving someone deeply gives you courage.

--Lao Tzu

CHAPTER 1: *Love is the Reason to Wake up Smiling*

I am alive because every day of my life someone somewhere has loved me.

My parents loved me enough to have me. They raised me, fed me, clothed me, educated me. They taught me the most fundamental things I know about love.

My friends loved me enough to save me. When, as a college sophomore, I had a stroke in the owner's box at a professional football game, they carried my paralyzed body carefully. They clapped their hands raw making sure I didn't fall asleep. They visited my bedside, sneaking in Sonic when I could no longer stand the hospital food. They did not laugh at the drool that dripped from a mouth I could not move.

My doctors loved me enough to rebuild me. Their therapists inspired me.

My wife loved me enough to give me a son. While our love changed shape--we are no longer together--Reece is living, breathing proof that love is generative, creative, and perfect in design. It is us humans who mess love up. Luckily, there's Communication to help with that.

My son loves me enough to hug me unprompted and at random moments throughout the day, making my heart swell and immediately dissolving life's frustrations. He continues to teach me that love is the reason to wake up smiling.

- *List three reasons in your life to wake up smiling:*

_____

_____

_____

_____

_____

_____

_____

_____

A Turning Point at the Turn of the Century

Having a stroke, especially at such a young age, is what transformed my perspective and galvanized the writing of this book. My stroke woke me up, shook me up, made me question the trajectory of a life I'd been taking for granted. For that reason alone, I am beholden to the shadow-thing that almost killed me. When my body turned traitor, my life turned around.

Even so, I would never wish the experience on anyone. I'd rather you instead read *Swinging Faster* and learn from the trials I navigated firsthand. For twenty bucks, you can have all the wisdom and none of the pain. I pretty much guarantee you that nothing else in life will come so easy.

Let me set the scene:

In 2000, a U.S. postage stamp cost 33 cents.

Mad Cow Disease was sweeping Europe.

Divers in Egypt had just discovered Cleopatra's palace.

The first sequence of the human genome was published.

Y2K was debunked and tech hysteria was subsiding.

I, Tommy Haydon, Jr., was twenty years old, a student at Texas A&M, and 110% ignorant of the deadly mass blossoming in my brain.

At 20, I didn't worry about my health. I worried about how many girls liked me. I worried whether the New Orleans Saints would make the playoffs. I worried in a somewhat more distracted fashion about my grades, which were terrible but largely unconcerning to me. The only thought I gave to my body was what it would look like shirtless on a beach in Cozumel: that year's Spring Break destination.

Health is funny like that. Unless you're a hypochondriac, without symptoms you have no cause to think anything is wrong. I was young, and in good shape. My best friends Kai and Ryan regularly met me at Gold's Gym at 5:00 AM to work out. We drank beer but never let the partying spiral out of control. I was a normal kid, fun-loving and responsible, just trying to find his way in the world.

Had anyone mentioned the word "stroke" then, I would have thought first of my golf game. 75 strokes, three-over-par! I love to golf; it is from a golfing metaphor that this book takes its title. Medical strokes, on the other hand, were something that happened to old people. Sagging faces, slurred speech, brain damage. What consideration had I for "oxygen deprivation"? *Nada*. I cared about chickens!

That's right, I was a Poultry Science major! I call it "Avian Science" because it sounds a bit better, but back then I was all about Ag Business. Today I'm a house-flipper with a real estate license and a financial advising certification, which has nothing at all to do with poultry. Unless of course you want to raise chickens on a ranch that I sell you--then I can help you in two ways!

The point is that people change. Our interests and priorities and even our deepest loves change. My focus changed three times: Engineering, General Studies, and back again. My girlfriends changed three times: Amy,* Beth*, and Claire*. I've been engaged twice and married once and held three professional positions. But everything I've done, I've done out of love. Every job has taught me something truer about people and passion. Every person I've loved and who has loved me in return has ushered me to the next level of human emotion.

Amy taught me to play guitar. She loved Janis Joplin and even looked like her: thin, with straight brown hair. "Soul" infused her every action.

Beth was my high school sweetheart. We got engaged after graduation, then broke up in college. The stroke brought us back together, for awhile.

Claire was blonde-haired, green-eyed, loud, and dominant. She took control, and I loved that about her. She was also very affectionate. Sometimes I wonder what it would be like to be with her today.

I was trying to break up with Amy when Claire came along, and then I was trying to break up with both of them when Beth re-entered the picture. I've never been great at confrontation when it comes to the women I'm dating, but I share what I've learned in Chapter 5!

Other than that, I played pick-up on the weekends, kept in semi-regular contact with my parents and older sister, enjoyed late-night pizza and went to class when I felt like it. As the theme song to *All in the Family* affirmed, truly "those were the days."

- *Where were you in 2000?*

_____

_____

_____

_____

_____

_____

_____

_____

_____

- *Who were you at 20?*

_____

_____

_____

_____

_____

_____

_____

_____

CHAPTER 2: *November 19, 2000*

So now you know a little bit more about who and what and where I was right on the cusp of the twenty-first century.

It was in the late fall of that year--November 19, to be exact (as if I could ever forget the date) that everything changed. Nothing in my life seemed that serious until the very fact of living was.

I suppose it could always be worse. I could have been on the toilet when the stroke hit, leaving someone to find me passed out with my pants down. That would be pretty embarrassing, right? As it was, my shadow-thing caught up with me in the middle of vacation, watching my favorite team pass some pigskin around on a Sunday afternoon in New Orleans.

On that day, the Saints were playing the Oakland Raiders. Our flight left College Station at noon Saturday and landed in the Big Easy 40 minutes later. As per usual, we started drinking 40 minutes after that.

Come Sunday, we were all a little hungover, nursing bottled water and Louisiana's finest Cajun in the Saints's owner's box. Around 2:00 PM, sometime in the game's third quarter, I suddenly felt sure I was going to faint. "Hey, man," I croaked to Ryan. "Can you get me another water?" I proceeded to drink the whole bottle he brought me before he'd even had a sip of his, so I grabbed his water and drank it, too.

Then I just slumped over into the empty seat next to me. Ryan had no idea what was happening, but helped carry me up the stairs to the landing where there was more room. Because I couldn't hold myself up, Ryan kept me propped up, and that's when a neurologist in the room recognized the signs of a stroke. She ran up the stairs, got in my face and started shouting "Don't go to sleep! Wake up, Tommy, don't go to sleep!" Every time I closed my eyes, she clapped louder. I felt sleepy, lethargic, and light-headed ... but no pain.

They rushed me to the hospital via the ambulance normally reserved for a hurt player. Once at Tulane Medical Center, they admitted me and immediately stripped me down. I'd thrown up twice, red beans and rice--a dish I loved but wouldn't be able eat for the next fifteen years after the stroke.

For what felt like forever, the staff left me lying stark naked on a gurney in a hospital anteroom. It was such an emergency that they'd just pulled me in and set me up in what was almost a nursery, with all the windows you'd peer through to see the babies. There was a curtain but nobody'd bothered to close it. They were too busy trying to figure out what was wrong, hooking me up, keeping me alive. Through the windows I could see my best friend's mom trying not to look at me.

All I knew was that I couldn't feel my body in space. I couldn't move, and I couldn't talk to say, "Hey, could you close that curtain?" By the time I regained partial feeling, I almost wished I hadn't. What followed was a barrage of tests and ballooning catheters so painful that I directly attribute the anxiety issues I have today to that experience.

■ *Describe a time something happened to you that was outside your control. How did you feel?*

_____

_____

_____

_____

_____

_____

_____

_____

_____

Diagnosing a Mystery

The first tube they stuck up my groin, through the femoral artery, snaking it all the way to my brain. Dye from the catheter flooded my system, revealing a brain bleed the size of a jumbo egg. Still unsure what had caused the bleed, they put me on a preventative anti-seizure drip called Dylantin, then sent Dr. Mascott to see me, my neurosurgeon and a personal friend of Mr. Benson.

Dr. Mascott took one look at the scans and diagnosed a not altogether-uncommon malady called an AVM, or arteriovenous malformation. Supposedly one in ten people have an AVM somewhere in the body, and whether it ever causes a problem depends on how large the mass grows and the degree of external pressure to which it is subject. The mass forms in-utero when two blood vessels accidentally collide and begin growing together. Because the skull is a rather inflexible cage, my AVM had no more room to expand. It burst; the extra blood choked my brain; I had a stroke.

Lucky for me, I was in the best hands in which I could possibly be. Dr. Mascott was so skilled at removing AVMs that he'd pioneered the Mascott Protocol, a procedure that, he went on to inform me, was really my only option-- unless I wanted the threat of another stroke hanging imminently over my head for the next decade, knowing full well another stroke might kill me. The Mascott Protocol, on the other hand, was two mere 7-hour surgeries that could either reduce my chances of another stroke to less than 1% ... or disable me permanently.

I had a day to decide, but there was really no decision to make.

- *What's the hardest decision you've ever had to make?*

_____

_____

_____

_____

_____

_____

_____

_____

_____

Full Steam Ahead

Of course I was scared. I was twenty years old! But I loved myself enough (or was stubborn enough) not to go down without a fight. If my body wanted to beat me up, I would swing faster, and we'd see who got to the punchline first.

Did I mention that I still couldn't move or speak? Forget verbal consent; words like "yes" or "no" were beyond me. I *blinked* my answers to the hospital staff for the better part of two days. Once I decided to have the surgery, the worst news yet came back to me: I was to wait, for another whole helpless, bedridden week.

The only way I got through that period was by surrendering to the obvious love of my family and friends. Despite divorcing when I was five, my mom and dad together boarded a plane to New Orleans as soon as they heard the news. They took shifts at my bedside, nearly liquefying their own brains with long days of mind-numbing television (the Bush-Gore recount was happening then) and longer nights of worry.

The girls--Amy, Beth, and Claire--also called, sent flowers, and/or visited me. Beth, my high school girlfriend, was the first to show; she drove from A&M to New Orleans the night she found out. Amy booked a flight for the following week. Claire--always the cooler head--respected my dad saying, "No, let's give it time." She waited to come see me until I was back in Austin, nearly a month after the initial stroke.

The hospital staff were also amazing. Realizing that I'd quickly grow depressed doing nothing but waiting, they started me on a vigorous therapy schedule to regain as much speech and motor control as possible before the surgery. I met with physical and occupational therapists twice a day, and the Wednesday morning after my stroke I woke up moving my big toe.

Mom was in the room with me at the time. She called the nurse, who came running. The nurse said, "That's great, Tommy! Can you move anything else?" I couldn't. I wiggled that toe maybe ten times and then I was completely worn out. Thursday I found I could move my foot. By Friday I could kind of turn my body. It wasn't exactly a miracle, but it was progress, and it was all the hope we needed.

In particular, those small but significant improvements (tiny miracles, really) bolstered me against my most opinionated critic: another neurologist on staff named Dr. Roberts*. To this day I don't understand his agenda, but

Dr. Roberts routinely went out of his way to warn me against the surgery. He loved to tout the risks of the Mascott Protocol over and over again, reminding me how close the incision would be to my optic nerve, that I could go blind. Tossing unfavorable percentages around seemed to be his favorite pastime, especially the 40-60% chance I had of *dying*. In my head I just kept repeating, "I'm ready. I'm gonna do it," and let the words of encouragement from everyone else around me drown out his petty naysaying.

As if to prove Dr. Roberts finally and utterly wrong, the day before surgery I won my most startling battle yet. I'd been practicing the motions of walking all week, watching in a mirror the way my left foot moved, and struggling to pattern my lame right foot after it. When my physical therapists told me we were going to 'walk' down the hall that afternoon, I knew they meant with a gate belt and a cane. The gate belt goes around your waist and allows a PT to hold you up--basically, to carry all your weight. We moved out of the room one step at a time and down the hall toward the elevators.

On the return trip, I was feeling strong and not a little overconfident. I asked the therapists to let go of the gate. They thought I was crazy, but they acquiesced. Then I handed them the cane. Both PTs braced themselves for my inevitable fall--which never happened. With agonizing slowness and a level of concentration that left me shaking, I walked around the corner and back into my room. I did it for Mom.

My mother does not cry, but she cried when she saw me walking.

We had a lot to be thankful for that Thanksgiving.

On November 28, 2000 Dr. Mascott sent another catheter from my groin to my brain and through it shot glue into the heart of my AVM. That was the first surgery; it took seven hours.

By the next day, the glue had hardened, temporarily coagulating the still-leaking blood and supposedly making the mass easier to remove. I guess I was special; the operation that should have again taken seven hours for me took almost fifteen.

When I woke up from surgery, I was paralyzed again.

- *Who inspires you to overcome the greatest odds?*

_____

_____

_____

_____

_____

_____

_____

_____

Ready for something scarier than paralysis? Try drug-induced dreams. You can't outrun them. They're waiting every time you close your eyes.

While under anesthesia in the operating room, I first had that uncanny experience of floating above my body. I remember looking down at myself on the gurney, watching Dr. Mascott and thinking I could leave the room if I wanted.

Later, being wheeled down the hallway, an IV in one arm and people to both sides of me, I had a vision that can only mean I was unconscious--and yet, conscious enough to recall it. Myself and the staff, we all loaded into an elevator. As I was lying on my back, I had no choice but to stare at the ceiling. Blood began to run down the walls of the elevator. It started building up like water. I remember panicking, thinking "If the blood rises over me, I'm dead." It did--it rose all the way up past me, then I heard the long *beep*: the sound when you die on the table.

I woke up two days later, having slept over 24 hours. My dad was in the room, watching Kansas State play Oklahoma in the Big 12 championship. Yes, my *dad*. I knew who *he* was; I knew who *I* was; by all rights, I'd come through brain surgery with no memory loss whatsoever. Of course, we'd soon realize that while my emotional memory was in tact, I'd completely lost the "memories" of how to talk and walk. But as I'd proven before, those could be regained. The important thing was I was alive! And not blind!

- *What small triumph in your life can you celebrate today?*

_____

_____

_____

_____

_____

_____

- *What abilities do you take for granted? Be grateful for them!*

_____

_____

_____

_____

_____

_____

_____

CHAPTER 3: *After the War*

I won't bore you with all the tedious details of my recovery. Suffice it to say that with the same stubbornness with which I approached an inherently risky surgery, I applied myself to occupational, speech, and physical therapy once more. Shortly before Christmas I was released from Tulane and transferred back to Austin, where I continued inpatient therapy at Health South for two more weeks. Right away in January 2001, I requested a transfer to outpatient therapy in College Station, so that I could resume classes at Texas A&M.

In retrospect it was far too soon, but I'd become impatient with living like a vegetable. My limbs were weak and uncoordinated. I couldn't pick up a glass. When I tried to eat or drink normally, it dribbled out my slack mouth. Worst of all I couldn't feel it. I registered pressure, and temperature differences, but my light touch receptors were fried. Even today if someone barely brushes me I can't tell, unless for example his hands are really cold.

So I hobbled around campus with a cane, fooling myself and no one else that nothing in my life had changed. To give you an idea just how bad it was: I straight up could not read. I don't mean comprehension and information retention--but actually reading, like recognizing words. I was a kindergartner in college.

As I improved, I reassumed more and more responsibility for myself. Over the summer I took classes at Austin Community College, so to make up some credits while staying close to home. In one class I wrote a paper on

"Strokes and Arteriovenous Malformations," in which I explained how "strokes can happen to anyone from birth to old age" and stressed the importance of a healthy diet and exercise. Having made it out of that hospital bed with my life, paying my story forward seemed a bargain price and a privilege.

I graduated Texas A&M three years later with a bachelor's degree and all my dignity. One thing's for sure: I did not do it alone. My doctors, my family, my friends, my professors--*they* made it possible.

- *Who could you add to your team to make it stronger?*

_____

_____

_____

_____

_____

_____

_____

_____

Graduation day, May 2003.

Sometimes the only way to move forward is to let go of the things and people holding you back. It's not a judgment on them ... it's a celebration of the self. It means you recognize and embrace your path despite occasional pain.

After my stroke, I thought I finally knew what my path was. I wanted a wife, a family. I wanted to experience that "other half" of life because I wanted the promise of a legacy. The stroke had scared me into one brutal realization: life is fragile and it's fleeting. There was still a chance, however small, that a second stroke could strike at any time, and as many of us do when faced with the fact of our own mortality, I wondered who would remember me when I was gone.

I said earlier that the stroke brought Beth and I back together. She was the first to my side at Tulane, and was absolutely responsible for me healing as quickly as I did. She chauffeured me to therapy appointments, fed me like a child before I could feed myself, and in every way had the patience of a saint. Therefore, ignoring all the warning signs of our previous break-up, I proposed to Beth a second time in January 2001. Our re-engagement lasted all of five months, before the stress of "dealing" with me in my condition became too much for her.

I tried reminding Beth it wouldn't be that way forever. "I'm still getting better," I said. "I'll soon be more independent." It didn't matter though, and in the end, it was for the best. Beth was nothing but honest with me, and completely entitled to her feelings. Why was I trying to convince someone to be with me who didn't want to do so? We both deserved more. Settling for anything less would be a disservice of the highest order: self-sabotage.

Instead I chose self-love. I dove even deeper into my therapies, determined to become as independent as possible as quickly as possible. While stacking and re-stacking endless piles of magazines (an activity my OT prescribed to refine motor skills), I worked through my disappointment to arrive, eventually, at forgiveness. You can't fault someone for not choosing you. You can't hate the person you loved just because they couldn't love you back.

Those emotions--love, and hate--are closer, I think, than we realize. Often we hurt the people most whom we love the most, and in turn feel the most hurt by them. At such times, it's easy to confuse love with hate ... but the 'hate' is really only misplaced hurt. Beth was my first love. Part of me will always love her, but we were never destined to be a success story.

Success requires communication skills I didn't have yet. I'll share those with you now in Part 2.

PART TWO
Communication

The single biggest problem in communication is the
illusion that it has taken place.

--George Bernard Shaw

Communication to a relationship is like oxygen to life:
without it, it dies.

--Tony Gaskins

CHAPTER 4: *The Two Types of Communication*

We're all familiar with the two main types of communication: verbal and nonverbal. Familiarity is not the same as intentionality, however, and it's the lack of intentional communication that creates communication breakdown.

By and large, verbal communication is intentional. To speak we have to think, to formulate a conscious question, statement, or reply. Even the times a phrase "slips out" that we wish we could take back--it is still the product of firing neurons, a well-oiled call-and-response machine systematically constructed from and influenced at any one time by old behavior patterns, the environment, duress, lust, fear, and a whole host of other factors, instinctual and intellectual alike.

Nonverbal communication, on the other hand, is almost always unintentional. That is, we cross our arms defensively, or move our hips into our partner suggestively, not because we consciously hope to achieve a certain effect, but because these are primal and *universal* human responses to standard stimuli. Such reactions must be consciously unlearned, *intentionally unpracticed*, in the same way one bites his tongue to intentionally withhold an inappropriate remark.

Because we can only change our communication habits by becoming aware of them, I ask that you read Part 2 with an inwardly-turned eye of scrutiny. Approach these scenarios not as thematic or psychological commentary but a guide to self-reflection. *Intentional* self-reflection.

■ *Brainstorm a list of verbal or nonverbal communication habits you've noticed in yourself or others. What effect do they have on relationships?*

_____

_____

_____

_____

_____

_____

_____

_____

Aphasia isn't Awesome, but It's Useful

You might be wondering what makes me the expert on communication. I'm laughing in my head right now; I'm hardly an expert. No degree in Poultry Science prepared me for a thesis on the human psyche. All the same, I've spent more hours observing human behavior than some licensed psychologists, given that after my stroke I had a little thing called aphasia.

Aphasia strictly afflicts your verbal communication. "A" means "without," "phasia" means "speech," and although the term covers a broad range of language disorders, for me it meant "the inability to recall words." First there was a period of a few weeks where I couldn't speak at all. Even after that, however, I'd be talking and suddenly forget the next word I wanted to say. I could see a picture of whatever it was in my mind, but I didn't know how to say the word. Still today I will get stuck once in a while.

An interesting thing happens when you can't speak. You begin to intentionally communicate with the eyes. There was the obligatory blink once for "yes" and twice for "no," but there was also that neglected twin: listening. Because I could not speak, I watched. I learned to listen with my eyes. I realized that sometimes people say everything by saying nothing. I internalized, and became intentionally aware of, forms of nonverbal communication from body language to eye contact that had never before registered with me as "speech." It made all the sense in the world when I recognized that nonverbal communication could be as or more powerful than verbal communication; after all, I couldn't speak, but I was hardly voiceless in that hospital bed. A fan of attention, I made sure everyone knew what I was thinking and feeling whether I could make my mouth form vowel sounds or no.

In some ways, I'd equate it to being an infant again. Babies acquire communication through observation, looking out at the world from a crib or a sling or a pair of arms instead of a gurney. There I was: a twenty-year-old man in a fetal position, learning to say "Mom" and "Dad" as if for the first time. In Austin my speech therapist would hold up a card with a picture of a red block and wait for me say "red." Full sentences, like "The block is red," seemed an insurmountable challenge. A couple wires got crossed a long the way, too: green and orange, for example. I know what orange looks like, I know what green looks like, but when I see green I say "orange." Grass is orange. I mean green! That still trips me up.

It's possible that the aphasia is permanent, especially as it relates to reading speed. Most of my vocabulary has come back, but the last IQ test I took revealed a seventh grade reading level ... all because I struggle to process visual inputs expediently. In a test where letters pop up on a computer screen, and I'm supposed to hit the space bar for every "X" before the next letter appears, I routinely score Low Average. Instead of reading, therefore, I listen to audio books! No problem!

All my aphasia really means is that communication has, for fifteen years now, been impossible for me to take for granted. When other people speak, I listen not to reply, but to understand. When I can't immediately think of the right words, I watch how other people react. I listen with my ears and my eyes and I intentionally choose the verbal and nonverbal cues that I present and to which I respond. Communication is a skill that has powerfully impacted my best relationships and made it easy to let go of those that do not serve me. As a skill, verbal communication can be practiced. Nonverbal communication can be unpracticed.

Let's get started!

■ *Pretend you've lost the faculty of speech for a day. In what other creative ways could you communicate?*

_____

_____

_____

_____

_____

_____

■ *Of these, are there any you might want to actually start using? Why/why not?*

_____

_____

_____

_____

_____

_____

_____

It's true: I used to despise confrontation so much that when I wanted to dump a girl, I manipulated *her* into dumping me first.

All you have to say is, "You know, we've been dating for awhile, but I'm just not feeling it anymore." Easy, right? WRONG. For the longest time, I was so worried about hurting the other person that in the end all I did was in fact hurt them--with my emotional dishonesty. You cannot go around pretending feelings you don't have in a personal relationship. [Professional relationships are completely different, and we'll talk about those in Chapter 6.] In personal relationships there should be no agenda other than two people's mutual happiness. Romantic, platonic, or familial, it never pays to 'fake it 'til you make it.'

My divorce was one break-up for which I never wished. For all my talk of mutual happiness and emotional honesty, I do believe that marriage is forever, a COMMitment in which COMMunication is essential. With enough open and respectful dialogue, and *intentional* nonverbal communication that underscores *Yes, I want to make this work*, even married people should not have to fake it.

Of course, at the risk of sounding cliche, communication really is a two-way street. Both people have to want it, to believe in it, and to practice it.

■ *Consider your closest relationship at this point. When you're honest with yourself, what agenda do you have for it?*

_____

_____

_____

_____

_____

_____

_____

_____

Crazy in Love

I met the woman who would be my wife when I was 23 years old. Monica* was 28, a baseball mom, and way, way out of my league. At the time, I was coaching Little League and her son John* was on my team. Every evening that Monica came to pick up John from practice, I watched her prance around in her tank top and jean skirt and thought, *If only I could be so lucky.*

My day job then was in real estate. A brand new agent, I was figuring out what it meant to fend for yourself in the shark tank. Monica had just finished her massage therapy training, and was finding the same: in 2003, Austin was an up-and-coming metro that would swallow you whole or spit you out based on who, not what, you knew.

One evening she approached me and asked if, seeing as we were both entrepreneurs, I might want to talk business over food sometime? Of course I said yes. The baseball mom and the baseball coach? It had all the makings of a long-term, grow-old-together relationship.

One extra-long lunch at Shady Grove later, Monica and I officially started dating. Within two months we were engaged. Everything was fast and intense and immediate and easy. I loved that woman like I've loved no one since. Married life--it's amazing. There is nothing more comforting than to have met and fallen unconditionally in love with someone with whom you expect to spend the rest of your life.

It's an awfully lonely life, though, if no one's communicating. Communicating includes both sharing and listening. In hindsight, it should have been a warning sign that Monica's favorite shirt read, "It's funny how you think I'm listening." All I have to say about that is ... we have the power to choose, and no power to escape the necessity of choice.

- *What influenced the last choice (major or minor) you made?*

_____

_____

_____

_____

_____

_____

_____

_____

_____

Honor Thy Father (& Mother)

Now that I'm a father, I understand just how nuanced the parent-child relationship can be. With the exception of a prerequisite rough patch in my teen years, I've always gotten along well with my dad. If you asked me how, I'd say it has everything to do with our communication style. In a few years more, I'll put it to the test with my own pre-pubescent son and maybe blog about it in *Swinging Faster Revisited*!

My dad is one of my best friends. We don't drink beer together and whine about our problems--it's not that kind of relationship. It's a familial friendship rooted in respect, wherein the body language we display to one another is more important than what we say.

For example, I occasionally get pissed at Dad, and he at me, but I would never, while I walk this green earth, raise a

Like father, like son.

fist to him or enter any physical altercation with him. I respect him too much for that kind of base interaction. In my family, character and integrity always trump temper. That's exactly the path I hope my son will choose.

Oh, we banter. Sometimes my dad will jokingly tease, "You know better than to try anything with me, anyway; I'll kick your ass!" My reply is always "You're 60 years old, I'm 35, and I could've kicked your ass ten years ago!" But we won't ever come to blows, no matter what he does, no matter what I do. There's nothing I wouldn't do for him or for Reece. I make sure to let both of them know it.

Reece just turned nine. He and I celebrated with a monster *Back to the Future* movie-watching session. In my house, fathers and sons value, respect, and love one another always. Reece might not yet understand the difference between "love," "unconditional love," and "in-love," but he will look back one day and know, by my words and by my actions, that I loved him unconditionally.

- *If you have kids, what values do you hope to instill in them?*

_____

_____

_____

_____

_____

_____

_____

_____

The Self-Reflective Partner

- -

Think about your last (or current) romantic relationship. Was it something you consciously sought? Did it "just happen?" Were you the aggressor or the pursued? Did you consent to--did you *choose*--the relationship, or was it more passive than that? Were you discriminate or profligate? If discriminate, based on what factors?

Come on, we all have our "ideal list" of attractive qualities in a potential mate.

■ *My ideal mate will have the following qualities:*

_____

_____

_____

_____

_____

_____

———————————————————————

———————————————————————

And now I have to ask--did you add "good communicator" to that list? Because:

> Commitment holds a relationship together.
> Communication brings it to life.

Successful communication goes one step beyond action. It means you don't just *do* or *feel* something and believe that's good enough, but you put in the daily work of self-reflection to understand your own actions and feelings, to take responsibility for them, and to be able to explain them to others. *Not* in the sense of justification--justification is less about communication and more a self-defense mechanism. Rather, self-reflection leads to self-improvement, which in turn allows you to show up fully for others, to be a dependable, engaging, communicative *partner* ... i.e. one who does his or her part.

And when we speak of "life partners," that's what we mean, right? Someone who shows up fully and actively contributes to the two-way work of a relationship?

Now let's revise that list. You've already determined you want A, B, C, D, and E in a mate. What if instead we talked about the qualities you don't want?

- *My ideal mate must <u>not</u> have the following qualities:*

_____

_____

_____

_____

_____

_____

_____

_____

Why did I ask you to consider the inverse of List 1? Well, people aren't actually ideal. Michelangelo's statues are ideal, but people are people, with all their messy neuroses and complicated desires; and if you didn't know it before, allow me to be the bearer of the light: no one that ever has existed or ever will exist was or will be made in your image, to your specifications, according to some checklist scribbled hastily in the middle of a book by Tommy Haydon, Jr.

I know ... breathe. It will be okay.

What this reality check means is that seldom will you find A, B, C, D, and E all in one person, and because on some fundamental level you know and accept that, it's tempting to begin to make exceptions. You meet someone and you think, "He has A, B, and E … but not C or D … but I guess that's okay because it's kind of formalist anyway, and after all … no one's *perfect*."

But, wait. Don't you deserve perfect?

Of course! (Provided you've put in the work of self-reflection and are an equally worthy partner). Therefore, if you instead approach relationships as, "I don't want G, H, and J," and you meet a cool guy who doesn't have G, H, or J, then all of a sudden you think, "Hey! This could work!"

And you never had to compromise on your list.

Use these parameters for life partners and employees, friends and service providers. In each case, the list of "must not have" qualities will change slightly, though they should all have one thing in common:

"Must not be a poor (or unwilling) communicator!"

Ask for Clarification

The key to weeding out the poor (or unwilling) communicators from your life is seeing through their camouflage! Luckily, there's a simple litmus test for good intentions, and it involves making a single observation: Does the person ask for clarification?

Whether or not an individual asks for clarification in a given situation forecasts everything about his/her partnership potential, because it instantly and accurately reveals the importance s/he places on communication.

People who ask for clarification *want* to understand others. They do not content themselves with generalizations, half-truths, or unfounded conclusions. They gather all the facts before passing judgment, thereby minimizing misinterpretations, faulty verdicts, and hasty write-offs. I hate to think how many relationships have ended because one person misunderstood the other, and instead of asking for clarification, chose to build an oft-irretractable reaction on the unsteady foundation of the almighty *paraphrase*.

Paraphrasing is what you do in English class. You paraphrase essays, books, and stories because the authors are generally unavailable to clarify their intentions. I once read a scholarly paper that successfully argued for Disney's overt sexualization of *Pocahontas*--a children's movie--entitled "Poke-her-hontas." Obviously anything, when either sufficiently decontextualized or subjected to a one-sided interpretation, can be spun antithetical to original intention. The only way to avoid such miscommunication is by saying to your partner, "Tommy, 'X' is what I felt when you said 'Y.' Can you tell me what you meant?" And by answering honestly when s/he asks you the same.

■ *Describe a time when failing to ask for clarification had either funny or disastrous consequences:*

_____

_____

_____

_____

_____

_____

_____

_____

_____

Disarm Spite

Most importantly, asking for clarification diffuses spite.
Good communication disarms spite immediately, as spite
is nothing more than--brace yourself--a *wholly unnecessary*
response to a *wholly unnecessary* misinterpretation.

Yes, spite is always the bridesmaid, never the bride. Spite is
always a reaction, never the action. When people act out of
spite, they are responding to something someone else did
that they *perceived* as being out of spite. Spite enters the
equation as a <u>reaction</u> to someone thinking that someone
else did something out of spite first.

In other words, people who act out of spite do so because
they never pause to reflect. Their actions are an immediate
reaction to a misperception--the misperception that
someone is being spiteful to them. Such people actually
generate the spite the first time.

No one likes to fight with spite. Just ask for clarification!

■ *Has a spiteful reaction (either your own or another's) ever hurt one of your relationships?*

_____

_____

_____

_____

_____

_____

■ *How might spite have been instead disarmed?*

_____

_____

_____

_____

_____

_____

_____

CHAPTER 6: *Communication & Professional Relationships*

In business, perceptiveness is a negotiator's best friend. If you can learn to more accurately read people, especially the nonverbal cues that may bely what's actually written between the lines of their verbal communication, you can dive deeper into an associate's or client's head than s/he can you, meaning you're already anticipating two steps ahead ... meaning you're going to close that deal or win that argument.

Professional pool sharks never take shots in isolation. They want to get the ball in the pocket *while* strategically lining up the next shot. In the same way, you want to correctly diagnose potential clients' personality types according to their verbal and nonverbal communication habits, because the rapport you build today is the long-term relationship you will reflect on tomorrow.

Chapter 6 introduces The Personality Spectrum, dissects The Handshake, analyzes Posture and Eye Contact, and concludes with one example of successful professional communication and one example of professional communication gone wrong.

The Personality Spectrum

Spectrums, by nature, span a range of variations, are bookended by extremes, and center around an average, or neutral fulcrum.

On the personality spectrum, the left and right "extremes" represent two common personality types between which all of us scatter.

On the left is the Dominant Driver. On the right is the Amicable-Stable individual.

LEFT		RIGHT
Dominant-Driver		Amicable-Stable
Craves being #1		Craves stability
Sales jobs or other non-stable income		Salaried jobs

There is no such thing as a "good" or "bad" personality type, and no type is superior or inferior to any other type.

That said, Amicable-Stable types on the right-end of the spectrum do tend to have inferiority complexes. They want the people with whom they do business to be superior to them, as that superiority makes the vendor the expert and is the reason they want to buy from the vendor in the first place. Conversely, in personal relationships Amicable-Stable types are most likely to mate with and have as friends other A-S types. They would not be comfortable so casually intermingling with Dominant-Driver types, who they see as being above themselves.

Dominant-Driver types meanwhile enjoy the feeling of superiority they get from surrounding themselves with Amicable-Stable types. They are more likely to dip into the right-end of the spectrum for both business and personal relationships, as Amicable-Stable types are less threatening to a D-D who wants to be in charge.

A Dominant-Driver can marry an Amicable-Stable and it'll work, so long as the Dominant comes to the Amicable side of the spectrum. The Dominant brings the stability that the Amicable craves. An Amicable who comes to the Dominant side on the other hand is in denial of his/her own wants, needs, and preferences. That relationship will likely be too unpredictable for an A-S to flourish. Two Dominants who both need to be #1 will butt heads. Two Amicables, on the other hand, are a great match. Amicables don't crave control; they are happy sharing the responsibilities and the decision-making. For the same reason, they are content allowing Dominants to control the things a Dominant needs to control.

- *Where do you fall on the personality spectrum?*

_____

_____

_____

_____

_____

_____

_____

_____

_____

Judge a Book by Its Cover

- -

Nonverbal communication includes handshakes and eye
contact--two great indicators of personality type provided
you interpret the signals correctly.

The handshake is usually the first physical contact you
make with a new acquaintance. Depending on the
circumstances of your meeting, the handshake may be
concomitant with or succeed earlier eye contact.

The following chart describes common handshake styles.
If you don't know what type of handshaker you are, shake
hands with someone naturally and ask them to identify
you.

- *My handshake type is:*

_____

_____

The Two-Pump

- "I'm going do what I want to because I love it."
- You're comfortable with getting paid a variable amount of income (not a salary position).
- A Driver type, you're going to do whatever it takes to be successful in the right way.
- Not a Dominant. You recognize that there are other ways to do things than you may know, and you can be persuaded to change your habits if you discover that the new way is a better way.
- You're also capable of admitting that the new way is better.
- You're to the point and direct; efficiency is key.
- Sometimes you pick your battles--most often in your personal life and/or with Dominant-Drivers. You'd be able to turn a battle with a gun into a battle with a pen with Amicable types.
- It would hurt your ego to continuously be on the losing end of a compromise. In that situation, over time you would say, "Forget this, it's a waste of energy."

The One-Pump

- One-pumps in general subscribe to about half of what two-pumps do.
- You have less of an 'edge,' especially when it comes to compromising. You're going to give up more in a compromise--or you might not even go into the compromise.
- You'll be able to lose more and still be okay; your ego won't be as badly bruised.

The Wrap-Around
• Very, very Dominant-Drivers. • U.S. presidents shake this way, especially Barack Obama. He winds up!
The Dead Fish
• Weak, limp, and acquiescing. • You prefer to let other people make decisions for you. • May still crave power, but the power is a facade granted to you by those to whom you defer.
Other
• This list is not exhaustive, and not every category will describe every person! You may have attributes from one or more columns, or none of these columns. Don't worry, it's just for fun--and if you learn something new, all the better!

<u>Eye Contact</u>
When we listen, we make eye contact a lot more than when we're talking, because we're absorbing information. We look away when we're talking because we're thinking, gathering information to convey to the listener, perhaps recalling memories.

Good listeners know the difference between concentrating and staring. People who concentrate on the speaker listen to understand and to reply. People end up staring when they drift off into their own thoughts--an occurrence made very obvious when the speaker suddenly pauses and you have no idea what s/he just said or asked you.

It's going to happen, especially if you find the speaker completely uninteresting. Where professional relationships are concerned, however, it's best not to let on or get caught in a stare.

Therefore:
1. **Be quick**. A lull in the conversation makes it appear as though you were not paying attention.
2. **Be retentive**. What did the speaker just say? What do you have to contribute to the topic?
3. **Be attentive**. Stay on topic. A quick topic change indicates disinterest.
4. **Be thorough**. Complete each thought.
5. **Be smooth**.When you stop talking and I start talking, there has to be a break in the action. I have to look off, to break that eye contact--otherwise,. it just becomes too awkward. Don't draw too much attention to the act of eye contact (and/or of breaking it), either.

■ *In addition to handshakes and eye contact, what other nonverbal cues do you find important for good communication?*

_____

_____

_____

_____

_____

_____

_____

_____

_____

Posture, Facial Expressions, & Self-Confidence

- -

Look at any non-posed portrait of any person, familiar or stranger--and you can immediately discern that person's level of self-confidence. The pose they naturally adopt, how they situate themselves in relation to others in the same shot, and facial expressions are all externally visible clues.

Imagine a photo of four young adults at a party. Maybe it's a mixer, a networking event, or a charity fundraiser. They're all well-dressed, carrying drinks or purses or briefcases. The woman to the far left, she's smiling but looks unsure of herself. Her shoulders are turned toward the camera and away from the group, indicating a distance from the others of which she may or may not be aware. She probably doesn't know them well, and she probably did not choose to be at the event of her own free will. Now she's rueing the fact that she has to be in a photo commemorating the event. Erica is an Amicable-Stable with a salaried job.

The guy to the far right is turned half to the group, half to the camera. He's not showing teeth, and may be irritated at being interrupted by the photographer. Tom is Dominant, but not a Driver. He shakes One-Pump style.

The remaining man and woman are in the center of the picture because they need to be the center of attention. They look relaxed and happy with big smiles, and would likely feel equally confident together or alone. Samantha and Jeff are Dominant Drivers. They probably have jobs that pay a variable amount of income and are bonus or commission-based.

■ *Find a recent group picture of yourself. What do your posture, facial expression, and position in relation to others say about your personality and/or self-confidence?*

_____

_____

_____

_____

_____

_____

_____

_____

The Condo Question

One last indicator of personality type (and a fun icebreaker to boot!) is The Condo Question.

In this hypothetical scenario, you've been given the chance to buy a beautiful and affordable beachside condo. The only decision you have left to make is whether you'd prefer to live on the first floor or the fifth floor. These are the facts:

1. A fifth-floor condo costs the same as a first-floor condo.
2. The fifth floor has a view of the ocean; the first floor has a view of the dune.
3. In the event of a fire, the first floor would be the first to evacuate; the fifth floor would be the last.

- *Which condo do you choose and why?*

_____

_____

_____

_____

_____

_____

_____

_____

First-floor people are practical and steady. They don't fluctuate a lot. They'll eat the same thing for breakfast seven days in a row because it fulfills a basic function. At a restaurant, they find a dish they like and they order it every time: that's why they go to the restaurant in the first place. First-floors vote more conservative than liberal, but might have a green streak. They're middle-class.

Fifth-floor residents need much more variation in schedule, routine, and meals. "Routine" may not even be a part of their vocabulary. They're socially and fiscally liberal, equally supportive of gay marriage, tattoos, piercings, and dangerous cars. They drive Corvettes or monster trucks and live at either extreme of the income spectrum: fifth-floors either have high-paying jobs with high risk, like money managers, or they're waiters making under $15/hour. They're upper-class or lower-class. They work hard, play hard.

Selling on the Spot

Sometimes a client (or a doctor or a vet or a hairdresser) is referred to you in advance, and you have time to prepare for the meeting. You know what you will say and what questions you will ask, and only infrequently will you find yourself caught off guard, forced to respond on the spot to something unexpected.

Other times, the doorbell rings while you're stepping out of the shower or the person in front of you in line to checkout randomly strikes up a conversation, and suddenly you sense the opportunity for a sale. In either case, you're unprepared and have to think on your feet. If you want it to go well, you're going to listen as much or more than you're going to speak--because you have a lot of information to gather in a short amount of time. You will gather it by observing both verbal and nonverbal cues, listening with your ears and your eyes, and **mirroring** the speaker. *You will stick the sale by reflecting the speaker back to him/herself.*

Here's a story of a time I successfully used professional communication skills to cement a business relationship. Given that I was only seventeen years old at the time, dear reader, take heart!

The high school I attended, St. Michael's, held an annual raffle fundraiser. Each student was supposed to sell thirty raffle tickets at $25 a pop. Any student who sold all thirty tickets got a day off from school.

On the Friday morning before the cut-off, I had twenty-six of thirty tickets left. By Friday afternoon I'd sold them all ... by selling to the people whom I knew had not been approached. Five tickets went to the guy who came to stock the Coke machines. Two to the A/C repair guy. One to the custodian (everybody forgets those people).

One unfortunate truism in business is that in general, salespeople only sell to the clients or customers with whom they are comfortable. A middle-class financial advisor, for example, may not feel comfortable selling to a client with a net worth of $3 million. A car salesman may not feel comfortable selling to a customer in a suit and tie who has clearly overdressed the employee.

The reason for their discomfort is clear, if illogical: fear. The financial advisor fears the client might move in circles beyond his area of expertise. The clerk fears that the customer is more of an expert than she. So they don't stick the sale. They lose it before they try.

Not even the desire for the dollar outweighs that fear. It doesn't come close! What businesspeople don't realize is that they could sell dirt to a worm if they only *mirror the client*.

1. If your client/customer talks fast, you have to talk almost as fast. Otherwise you risk losing his respect: he's not going to think you're smart enough to handle what he needs handled.
2. Let him dictate the handshake. Is the handshake weak or strong? Three pumps or one?
3. When working with Amicable-Stables, talk slower.
4. Don't underdress someone on the right end of the spectrum. He won't be impressed.
5. Don't overdress someone on the left end of the spectrum. A Dominant-Driver will find your presumption to be confrontational and competitive. Shoot for a "close second" that indicates you're still good enough to do business with. [*See page 56 for the spectrum.*]

Accurately reading nonverbal communication cues allows you to more competently mirror your clients, your spouse, or your mortgage lender: anyone you need on your side. When you ignore the cues, you run the risk of failing resoundingly, like Sarah*. Sarah is a fellow real estate agent who one night found herself presented with an unexpected opportunity.

Sarah and I went to dinner in Austin. Our waitress that night was very cool. All three of us were talking and joking and it came out that the waitress was about to get her real estate license. Of all the industries out there, to find three REALTORS® at one booth seemed pretty incredible.

Sarah decided to capitalize on the opportunity. "I'll introduce you to my broker," she told the waitress. "It's tough in this industry. Email me, I'd love to sit down with you, see if I can help you out."

She should have stopped there, based on the waitress's nonverbal cues. The woman had stiffened and turned her shoulders away from Sarah, clearly uncomfortable with what must have felt to her like an unwanted intrusion. The waitress thanked Sarah but her initially bubbly personality had cooled considerably. She took Sarah's card without further comment.

When the waitress returned with our appetizers, Sarah continued what was by this time becoming a full-on sales pitch. I could tell that the waitress only wanted to get away, but Sarah had no clue. She wasn't paying any attention to the woman's bold body language or shifting eye contact. As Sarah was irritating even me, I doubt that waitress will ever contact her.

It was a perfect example of that old cliche: "You give 'em enough rope, they hang themselves." Sarah's obliviousness cost her a networking opportunity that night. Sarah did not mirror her client. She could not grasp the fact that communication breeds success.

■ *In what situations might mirroring spur more successful interactions for you?*

_____

_____

_____

_____

_____

_____

_____

PART THREE
Success

Success is not final, failure is not fatal.
It is the courage to continue that counts.

--Winston Churchill

Success is a journey, not a destination.

--Arthur Ashe

CHAPTER 7: *Define Success ... Then Go after It*

Lately I've been thinking about what it means to have a successful life.

Is "happiness" a synonym for success? What constitutes happiness? Money? Self-worth? A great relationship?

What if you make lots of money but hate your job--is that still success?

If your job is your passion, but it pays next to nothing and you can't afford a nice car, a big house, or kids--are you successful because you got one thing (a very important thing) right?

The most genuine conclusion I keep coming back to is that success is more subjective than objective, that there cannot be one textbook definition for everyone. A student who earns anywhere between 70% and 100% on an exam is successful; he passed that test. Is the A+ student *more* successful? Well, it depends on what he wants to do with his life, and "wants" are subjective.

I "want" to have a successful life *every day* of my life. For me, that means enjoying my son; finding fulfillment in my work; and being financially free. With each new day, I have a new opportunity to do all three. By taking life one day at a time, I've learned to keep success a journey instead of some superficial, dead-end destination.

It used to be that I was destination-oriented. I thought that only perfection could be success, and so I held myself to impossible standards and berated myself when I "failed" to meet them. If, as the high school quarterback, I threw 20 times, I strove for 20 completions. Only a perfect game would have meant I was successful. Anything less was a fail.

Now I realize that the *only* way to be successful *is* to fail. You can't be successful at everything ... and if you haven't failed then maybe you're not successful at all. If you never were knocked down, you've never had to get up, and success is about getting up after failure. I look back on my life and I think, I failed here, and I failed here, and I failed here. What happened afterward? I got up, I dusted myself off, and I did better the next time.

■ *How do you define success?*

_____

_____

_____

_____

_____

_____

_____

_____

You might find it enlightening and affirming, as I have, to categorize the major events of your life as Failures, Successes, and Guarantees, with an emphasis on transforming Failures into Guarantees of Success.

For example:

I **failed** at marriage. BUT. I **succeeded** at bringing a perfect new life into the world, and I **guarantee** that I will give him every opportunity to find his own success.

I failed at being a financial advisor. BUT. I succeeded at returning to the work I love best--flipping houses--and I guarantee that I will run a fair and honest business.

I failed at becoming a millionaire. BUT. I succeeded at turning a profit on all 33 of the properties I've helped renovate, and I guarantee that both my client base and profit margin will continue to grow.

Guarantees are promises you make to yourself and others. As with all promises, all you can do is your best to see them through. If you fail again, you chart a new path to success and you again stay the course.

> Success is not final, failure is not fatal.
> It is the courage to continue that counts.

We've talked about forgiveness in relationships ... remember to also forgive yourself.

■ *No matter how practical or dreamy the goal, if you failed to achieve it, where did you succeed instead, and what will you guarantee in the future?*

_____

_____

_____

_____

_____

_____

_____

_____

The final two chapters of this book 1) examine some common qualities of successful individuals and/or relationships, and 2) offer my personal tips for living a successful life every day of your life, keeping in mind that:

**Love makes Communication possible.
Communication breeds Success.**

CHAPTER 8: *Common Qualities of Successful People*

Empathy. Persistence. Obstinacy. Resourcefulness. Gratitude. Learn 'em and live 'em!

Empathy

Empathy and sympathy. Do we need a refresher on the difference?

Empathy is the ability to understand and share the feelings of another. When you empathize, you "put yourself in that person's shoes."

Sympathy is feelings of pity and sorrow for another's misfortune. When you sympathize, you recognize a tragedy but do not personally relate to it.

Empathy is infinitely more important in relationships, personal or professional, than sympathy, because empathy forms the backbone of the shared human experience. More than someone feeling sorry for us, we need to know we are not alone ... that others have gone before us, paving the way for our sometime-failures and our more spectacular successes, inspiring us to rise again, and what is more--to extend a hand and pull still others up with us.

Empathy can exist because we are conscious creatures. Insofar as consciousness sets the human race apart, empathy has the potential to braid together the threaded spirits of all humankind into one unstoppable force. We can use that power for change and achievement, or to take advantage of others precisely when they are most vulnerable.

Let's use the example of Mike and Dave. Mike and Dave are two equally qualified and excellent employees of a local tech company. For five years, the two have chatted at the water cooler and made coffee runs together. Both would call the other a friend. On the morning that Stephanie announces her retirement, Mike and Dave find out they'll be competing for the promotion. Without a backward glance, Mike goes rogue. Rather than rely on his work ethic, strength of character, or performance record to earn the job, Mike lets leak several damaging rumors about Dave. He uses his 'friend' to get what he wants, never once putting himself in Dave's shoes.

At this point, one of two things will happen: either Mike will get Stephanie's old job, rewarding and reinforcing his back-stabbing behavior; or Dave will get the job anyway. No matter what, Dave will always know what type of man Mike really is. If Dave wins, he will never look at Mike for promotion. In fact, he might look to Mike for the first chance he gets to fire someone.

Had both men fought fairly for the position, the winner of the match would be quick to help out the loser--his equally qualified friend for whom he feels empathy. In this scenario, should Dave win he will promptly promote Mike, recognizing that Mike deserved the job as much as he. The win-lose outcome of the first scenario becomes in this case a win-win.

Life presents you with unexpected opportunities all the time, and every time you have a choice. You can step on the person in front of you, counting their failure as your success; or you can ask the person who's already where you want to be how she got there, and if she can help--with an appeal to your shared humanity.

It seems to me that today two things get in the way of empathy. The first is that we live in a throwaway society. Instead of fixing the broken blender, we toss it. It's a bad habit that by extension has us walking away from broken relationships. Why fix it when you can buy a new one? Divorce is easier than marriage counseling, and quitting a job more convenient than fighting for fair treatment.

The second challenge to empathy has to do with the way we've removed people from the human equation.

A few days ago I went into a bank where I keep an infrequently-utilized account. I only visit that bank when I need a big check to close on a property, so I don't know the tellers well except to have noticed every time they try to sell me on something. That day, it was mobile banking. "You wouldn't have to come into the bank ever again," the teller gushed, then blinked at my silent stare.

It's not her fault; she couldn't have known that I really like going to the bank. Not her bank, maybe, but my other bank, where the manager laughs at my jokes, approves my checks without holding them, and has become a real friend. I said earlier than COMMunication is essential for COMMitment, but the same goes for COMMunity. Whether due to technology or apathy, we've in large part lost any sense of human community. We socialize through computers instead of countenances, and in the midst of information overload forget how to feel anything at all. Empathy is being phased out in the desire not to hear, but to be heard. All the blinking, flashy, sound-bites drown out real communication--and without communication, we cannot achieve the glories for which we were meant.

We were put here to co-habitate on a very intimate level. Relating is the action, empathy the reaction, success the goal. The best way to get where we're going is to help others get where they're going.

■ *Who in your life could use a little empathy, and how might it benefit you both?*

_____

_____

_____

_____

_____

_____

_____

Had you asked me, as a child, where I was going, I would have said straight to the White House. I reckoned I was meant to walk with presidents and kings, to lead nations ... at the very least, to test my skills at the White House bowling alley or play hide-and-seek in its 132 rooms. When I grew up, I wanted nothing less than to be President of the United States of America.

While that dream has somewhat faded, should I decide to campaign I know for a fact that my lobbying skills are on point! Persistence is the second greatest quality of the successful, and it was persistence that made another dream of mine come true: attending Texas A&M as a Fightin' Texas Aggie!

Like most high school seniors, at seventeen I was itching and anxious to get out of the house. I'd planned for so long to attend A&M that my application materials were in well before even the early bird deadline, including an essay I felt sure would knock the admissions counselors off their feet. An athlete, a decent student, and a Relay for Life volunteer, there'd never been a stronger college-bound shoe-in.

Six weeks later, I received my rejection letter. No explanation; just the stock "We regret to inform you ..." nonsense.

Now, there's a difference between entitlement and persistence. I'm not going to say I *deserved* to get in more than the next student, but something certainly can be said for not giving up.

First I called the admissions office and spoke to a counselor directly. At his advice, I retook the ACT and requested reconsideration.

When I hadn't heard anything by December, I decided it was time for the big guns.

I still have a copy of the letter dated January 27, 1998 that I sent to Dr. Bowen, then president of the university. In it, I described a childhood spent watching A&M alums Lance Pavlis and Bucky Richardson play football on Saturday afternoons, and the fire I'd always felt to represent that fine university. I didn't beg, but I reasoned, noting everything that my "superb" personality would add to the student body.

After sending it, I checked the mail every day for a reply the way a child sneaks down the stairs to check the living room for Santa Claus--that is: giddily, hopefully, but not without a twinge of doubt. When I received my invitation to orientation, I thought it had to be a mistake--but the notices had crossed en route, and my acceptance letter came the following day. I pinned the letter to my bulletin board where I looked at it every day, beyond excited and still a little beyond belief.

You have to believe that anything is possible. Maybe next, I'll campaign for president.

January 27, 1998

Mr. President:

I know writing a letter to you instead of an admissions counselor is a bit unusual, but I feel that you should be informed of this situation that I am involved in.

I have wanted to attend Texas A&M University for as long as I can remember. I watched Lance Pavlis and Bucky Richardson on Saturday afternoons and that started my dream. As years past the fuel that kept that fire burning wasn't just football; it was Texas A&M University. Now my fire is beginning to die out.

On Monday, September 1, 1997 my application arrived first thing in the morning. About six weeks later I received a letter rejecting me completely. I understand that this happens to many students. Nevertheless, I tried everything I could in order to get my application reviewed again. I met Larry Perez of Admissions Counseling, I took the ACT again, I wrote a letter to the Admissions Office stating my thoughts. I was instructed by Mr. Perez to write the letter (attached). He told me that it might introduce something new in my application. Well I mailed the letter almost two months ago. I have not received a response.

I called A&M one morning a couple of weeks ago to ask about provisional school. I was told by Mr. Perez that provisional was reserved for students with lower educational backgrounds. I accepted that...until today when I heard that a friend of mine got a letter stating his provisional qualifications. This person goes to a private school similar to mine across town. Obviously provisional isn't just for lower educational backgrounds.

When I returned home I called Mr. Perez and informed him of this and he told me that they send letters stating that a person has been certified for a spot to compete for provisional acceptance based on consistency or certain information that might leave an indication of success. He also said that they didn't want anyone who they thought was not prepared. I then asked him why I didn't get a chance to at least compete for a spot in provisional school considering I go to St. Michael's College Preparatory School. His response was and I quote, "Write a letter."

I know that reviewing applications is not an easy job and I feel that I have been cheated in a way. I know that I can succeed and there are plenty of indications that I can do so. Every aspect of my high school career has been above average. I don't believe that it is fair to simply send me a letter of rejection without even looking at the rest application. I know that happened because Mr. Perez told me that himself. I feel that I should be given a chance at provisional school because my application is more than superb.

I thank you for the time you took to read this, ~~I appreciate it very much.~~

Thank You,

Tommy L. Haydon Jr.

Tommy L. Haydon Jr.

An early draft of the letter I sent to President Bowen. Keep in mind I was seventeen years old; I didn't think to preserve a clean copy!

■ *Describe a time you worked persistently to prove to yourself or others that anything is possible.*

_____

_____

_____

_____

_____

_____

_____

_____

Obstinacy

Obstinacy takes persistence once step further. The obstinately successful person never gives up because he is stubborn, and he's stubborn because he thinks he's right. It's a bit narcissistic in that way, but then obstinacy is what saved my life.

You ask a 20-year-old to make a potentially life-or-death decision like whether or not to have open brain surgery, he's always going to do things his own way. We teach our kids not to be stubborn; to listen; to only make mistakes once. As much trouble as my obstinacy has gotten me in over the course of my life, it's the reason I still have a life-- and an amazing one at that.

I spoke to my sickness like the adversary it was: with fightin' words! "Mo@#%&f#^*er, I am going to beat this sh*t, and go on with my life!" Call me any name you want, but don't tell me I can't do something I want to do. I'll prove you wrong.

Obstinacy also helps you get you your way more honestly than bribery, threats, or force--tools I do not recommend to the budding hero or heroine. While in outpatient rehab at Health South in Austin, a conversation with my therapist went something like this:

THERAPIST: "We'll do occupational, speech, and physical therapy once a day, and we'll see when you can get out of here."
ME: "I'll be out of here in a week."
THERAPIST: "No one's ever been out of here in a week."
ME: "Well, I am. And here's the other thing. We're going to meet twice a day."

I worked for three hours every morning and three more every afternoon. I treated therapy like a job. It was closer to two weeks before I was discharged, but I matched the clinic's record for quickest recovery ever. That's a success story.

- *When/how has obstinacy helped you get your way honestly?*

_____

_____

_____

_____

_____

_____

_____

_____

Resourcefulness

And then there are the delicate situations that require a little more finesse than obstinately bullying your way toward the goal. Resourcefulness is a skill that, like communication, can and should be practiced. It begins with taking stock of the situation, brainstorming as many alternatives as you can, picking that option with the highest chance of being realistically successful, and making your move!

For me, the goal was going seizure-free after my stroke. Whether it was lingering damage from the initial brain bleed, or trauma incurred during surgery, something caused my body to start suffering seizures about five months later. April 4, 2001 was my first grand mal. It happened at Beth's house, probably scaring her as much or more than me. The seizures continued at unpredictable intervals until January 2003, when I finally decided enough was enough. The pills my doctor had given me obviously weren't helping, so I wrested back the reins.

In January 2003 I was coaching youth basketball. One day in the middle of a game I felt another seizure starting. I motioned to the athletic director, ran out of the gym, and made it halfway around the building before I succumbed. The next day I called the clinic at Dartmouth University, where I'd learned they were performing an experimental but promising procedure on epilepsy patients.

Dartmouth booked my appointment; I booked a flight. Afraid my family would try and talk me out of it, I didn't tell anybody until the last minute. Right before I left I let my dad know. Not only did he support my decision, he said he would go with me. "Let's make a long weekend of it," he offered. "We'll fly into New York, spend a couple days in the city, then train up to Hanover." That's exactly what we did, and we had a great time doing it.

At Dartmouth, the first thing the doctor asked about was which seizure medications I'd already tried. Though I'd been on six different kinds, he didn't feel my sample size was big enough. He couldn't in good faith recommend me to the trial, so he wrote me a prescription for Lamictal instead. "Call me in 6 months," he said, and left the room.

I was devastated. The world's leading neurologist had just denied me my last hope for being both pill- and seizure-free.

Because between pills and seizures the pills were the lesser evil, I did start taking Lamictal. 300 mg daily. When it actually worked, I ate my crow--and happily.

Lamictal worked so well that in 2007 I declared myself "cured." I hadn't had a seizure in four years. Surely it meant that my brain had healed; it had nothing to do with Lamictal. Without consulting any medical professional, I slowly weaned my body off the drug over the next three years.

On August 19, 2010, I had the most severe grand mal of my life. Finally I learned to appreciate the pills instead of taking them for granted. Now I take one pill a day, and will every single day for the rest of my life ... barring some other advancement in the medical field. You can trust that I'll be doing my research, forever on the look-out for newer and better options. I'm just resourceful that way!

■ *Brainstorm a list of resourceful alternatives for any problem with which you are currently struggling.*

_____

_____

_____

_____

_____

_____

_____

_____

Dad and me (then 22) at the top of the Empire State Building.
It was negative three degrees in New York!

Gratitude

Although another pill was not the solution I'd hoped to find at Dartmouth, Lamictal was a blessing in disguise. It's painless, with a low side effect profile, and it *works*.

Successful people are (or should be!) grateful people. In the grand scheme of things, we can only control the controllables. For the wonderful parts of my life that I had no real hand in creating, I am eternally thankful.

There's a video of me from before my stroke. In it, I'm walking around and dancing in Cozumel. The difference between how I moved then and how I move now is more than noticeable; it's sad. Then I moved with the grace of a quarterback. Now I hip-swing my right leg, and roll my ankle any time I jump out of the car too quickly. I've also never relearned to play the guitar. My left fingers can no longer fret, and even if I played right-handed, they can't strum, either.

That said, odds were I was never going to walk again at all. When I look at it that way, I cherish that hip-swing. It's a Haydon hallmark now. Watch out world, here I come!

- *Name your "blessings in disguise." Be thankful for them!.*

_____

_____

_____

_____

_____

_____

_____

_____

CHAPTER 9: *Tips for Achieving Success*

In Chapter 8, I shared five common qualities of successful people. Chapter 9 offers five tips for living a successful life every day of your life, beginning with this book's titular lesson:

Swinging Faster

You've probably heard the adage "Work smarter, not harder." Because I believe the sentiment applies to more than just work, but also to leisure, relationships, and self-improvement, I've modified it using my favorite golf analogy: *Swing faster, not harder.*

The difference between successful people and unsuccessful people is that success-seekers are motivated by results. They care less about the precise method used to achieve the results, and more about achievement itself. I don't mean to suggest that we should all run out and, morals be damned, use any shady means we can to get at the goal. What I'm saying is that a too-narrow focus on technique can slow down or even muck up results that with a little resourcefulness, could be achieved faster and more easily. Don't get bogged down in the details, but keep the endgame at the forefront.

Some golfers swing as hard as they can. They've rationalized that a harder swing will send the ball farther, and insofar as the point of the pasttime is to get the ball onto the green, they figure--the harder the shot, the longer the shot, the fewer the shots. Those golfers are all caught up in the method. What such players don't understand is that with speed, not strength, comes power. A fast swing will drive the ball further than a hard swing, and you'll typically have better placement control as well. Better placement sets you up for fewer chips and putts; you're more likely to make par; and that's a successful game!

In business and in relationships, I keep the focus on what I want to achieve, allowing room for spontaneity, play, and best practices to emerge--the equivalent, in any situation, of swinging the best (the fastest) way. This propensity earned me the nickname "Donald Trump, Jr." ... because whenever I apply the Swinging Faster principle, I'm always successful.

■ *In what areas of your life should you swing faster, not harder? Are you results- or methods-oriented?*

_____

_____

_____

_____

_____

_____

_____

_____

Perfecting my game from 130 yards out

I just advised you to focus more on results than methods. For those who do need a little more direction in their methodology, however, to obtain those desired results, here's a good one:

Listen for the Light Knocks

First, we need to talk about giving up the myth of the Self-Made Millionaire. The Self-Made Millionaire is a pretty little invention designed to rival the likes of Bigfoot and Rumpelstiltskin. It's a story that entertains, and maybe even inspires, but it's fiction through and through. No elf-man split himself in half upon stamping his foot in rage ... and no Reed College drop-out built a personal computer empire single-handedly. [Steve Jobs was the brains of Apple, and remains its face post-mortem, but even Jobs was quick to credit all those who who helped him along the way.]

In the event that *Swinging Faster* makes me a millionaire (a guy can dream), shall I call my success self-made? I created and own the intellectual property; I should therefore be solely privy to all the attendant rights and privileges, no?

Well, let's not forget my ghostwriter. She was a step. The person who introduced me to my ghostwriter was a step. The team of people who kept me alive after my stroke, so that I could even be here to write this book--they were a step. Had I not had a stroke, my dad and I wouldn't have been sitting in a hospital room bored out of our minds, prompting him to say, "I'm halfway through my real estate courses; why don't you come back with me and we'll be

REALTORS® together?" cementing our relationship and giving me the real estate experience that underpins some of *Swinging Faster*'s lessons. In the end, all these people made me a (still hypothetical) millionaire. It would be ridiculous and egotistical to say otherwise. We need to give each other that credit.

In my wallet I carry a paper check made out to myself in the amount of $1,000,000. It's not the kind of check you cash; it's the cash against which you check your own success. That check is my talisman, a reminder both of my goals and all the people who make my success possible.

Every new relationship is an opportunity for success. The people who move in and out of our lives ... such encounters are not pre-determined, but manifested. When you put out into the universe that you need X to happen-- and it happens--then opportunity knocks. Sometimes it's a gentle tap and sometimes, because you're not paying attention, a heavy pounding. Listen for the light knocks. Let in those who want to help you.

■ *What lightly-knocking opportunities have you been ignoring for too long?*

_____

_____

_____

_____

_____

_____

_____

_____

_____

Invest in People
- -

And for gosh sakes, pay it forward! Show up for other people that they may have the time and energy and desire to show up for you!

What does it mean to "show up?" It means 1) **investing** time; 2) **challenging** your business partner or spouse; and 3) actively working toward the creation of a **legacy**. Your legacy is a gift you leave behind for other people, and whether tangible or immaterial, it better be a good one-- it's a final thank you to all those who made you a (financial, spiritual, or familial) "millionaire." More on that in a minute!

Time is a precious commodity. A non-renewable resource. It really matters how and with whom you choose to spend time, but like the money market, time can be a profitable investment. It accrues interest and value and hopefully one day you get a huge return. The best way to ensure a time investment's ultimate success is to treat it with the same respect reserved for other people. Be punctual, reschedule only when you absolutely have to, communicate clearly, and keep your word. With time (see what I did there?), your bicycle wheels will even out. This is my bicycle analogy:

Think of it like those old-school bicycles, the ones with a big front wheel and tiny rear wheel. The old-school bicycle represents any brand new relationship, business or personal. In such a relationship, each partner respects the other's knowledge, area of expertise, and/or level of life experience. Even so, each is hesitant at first to trust in the other person, given that factors like character, integrity, and reliability, when not upstanding, can jeopardize ability. On an old-school bicycle, knowledge is the big wheel and trust is the little wheel.

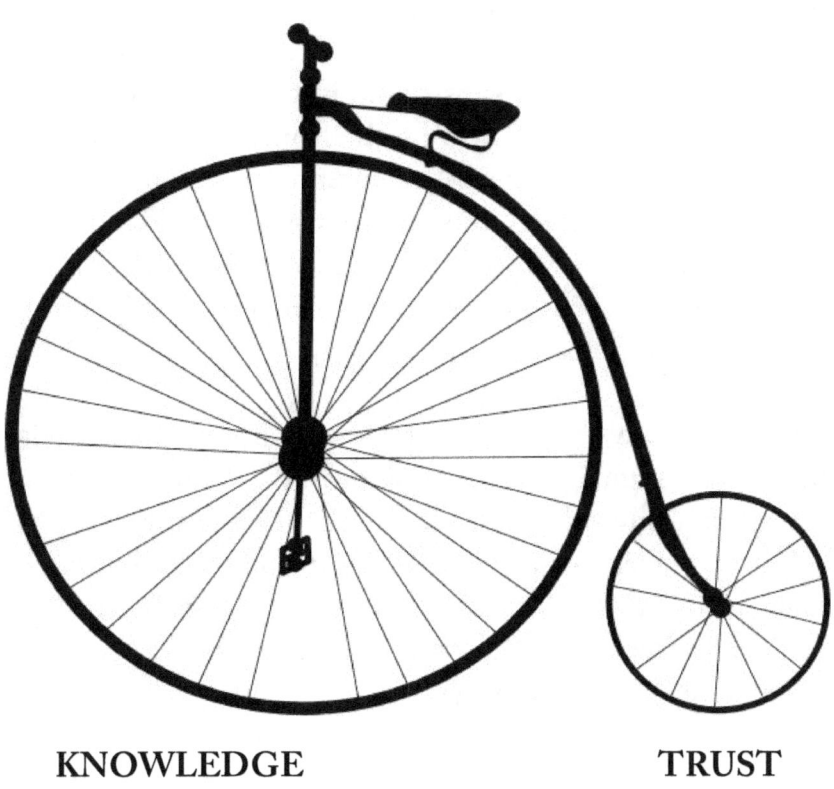

KNOWLEDGE   **TRUST**

Clients have only to look at my house-flipping history to know I'm a knowledgable contractor with significant experience. My big wheel in their eyes is gigantic. The rear wheel is proportionally minuscule, however, because unless they were personally referred to me, they have no reason to trust me. It's up to me to earn that trust, which I do by investing time.

It's been said that "people don't care how much you know until they know how much you care." Over time, the small wheel grows bigger and bigger until both wheels are the same size. At that point, you trust the other person's ability and intentions wholeheartedly; communication improves; and the relationship has every chance to succeed. Both people have chosen to "show up" maximally.

Other concepts can be substituted in the bicycle analogy. In some personal relationships, the front (larger) wheel might be a baggage wheel. You enter a relationship knowing your partner has an ex-spouse and a kid, but as the trust wheel grows you decide you can live with that baggage, even love it--after all, that person's history made him/her into the person s/he is today.

The reason why that old bike style isn't around anymore is because the functional design improved as two-wheeled transportation evolved. We found that bicycles with balanced wheels converted pedaling into motion more efficiently, and the same can be said of relationships: balanced wheels conduct forward momentum in sustainable, productive ways.

By the same reasoning, you should challenge your business partner or spouse or any other counterpart in any professional or personal relationship to also, like the bicycle, continue evolving. Be open to their constructive feedback, as well! Challenging your partner is a further investment of your time and it says you aren't 'settling' for a less than fully-realized relationship. You challenge because you care, because you want the best for your partner and for yourself.

A challenge can take any form from making your partner feel better after a bad day, to sitting down and really talking through a complex issue. Maybe your spouse just started a new business, and now that it's tax time, s/he owes $4,000. You offer to help them figure it out, you challenge them to think outside the box, so they don't have to go through it alone. If you're not challenging your relationships, or when you no longer care to attempt the challenge ... it's a sign that relationship is pretty much over. You've stopped "showing up."

Not showing up leaves a quitter's legacy. I choose every day to show up. This book I wrote, the business I've built, the son I'm raising ... all these will define my legacy. Legacy begins with the birth of a person or an idea, goes dark with death, and lives again with each recollection. It's what you leave behind: the gift that keeps giving.

I remember the day that Reece was born. I had on a red short-sleeve button-up shirt, jeans, and a baseball cap they made me replace with a scrub hat to go inside Monica's room. I didn't watch the C-section; I stood by her head, held her hand, and helped her bring our son into the world. That day, Reece made five generations of the Haydon clan. Before "Big Mammaw" (my great-grandmother) died, we took a photo of her, my grandmother, my dad, myself, and my son in the backyard. Even though Big Mammaw has passed, that photo still sits on the mantle, reminding me every day what it means to show up, and to leave a legacy of which I am proud.

- *How do you want to be remembered?*

_____

_____

_____

_____

_____

_____

_____

_____

Consult Your Board of Directors (Often)

I was still a financial advisor when my stepdad Perry died in 2010. I'd never delivered a death benefit claim to a client until I had to deliver one to my mom. She called me at 6:00 AM on a Tuesday, screaming, "Perry's not breathing!" Although I jumped in the car immediately, by the time I got to their house the paramedics had already draped his body with a tarp.

At Perry's funeral, I gave the eulogy. My speech was a confession and a call to arms. In it, I explained how Perry was on my Board of Directors, though I'd never gotten around to telling him. "My 'Board of Directors,'" I told the assembly, "is an on-call summit of the best and most influential people I know. They sit at a table and govern the company I call my life. Anytime I have a decision to make, I consult them in my head, watching, listening, and learning from the way they hash out alternatives and set action goals. They're my conscience and my guardian angels. Today, Perry truly is an angel."

Do it, right now: envision your Board of Directors. Then go out and thank those people in real life for contributing to your success. Do it before you lose the opportunity, like I did.

■ *Assign five people to your Board of Directors. Then let them know.*

_____

_____

_____

_____

_____

_____

_____

_____

_____

Become the Exception

Congratulations, dear reader.

You've made it this far ... not to the end, because the work--your work and mine--continues.

I hope you learned something useful, something you can implement in your life *today*, to more deeply love, more effectively communicate, and more rapidly find real success in your personal and professional relationships.

Remember,

> Love makes Communication possible.
> Communication breeds Success.

Toward that end, I leave you with a final directive: forget all these "rules."

Become the exception to the rule.

Good luck.

About the Authors

At the age of 20, **Tommy Haydon, Jr.** suffered a debilitating stroke that left him unable to walk or talk. It took a month in the hospital and 6 months of outpatient rehab for Tommy to regain mobility and relearn how to communicate. Fifteen years later, Tommy still can't play the guitar or walk without a hip-swing, but he is nevertheless proof of the power of positive thinking. When you can't talk for months, you listen, observe, and learn. In his first book since the stroke, Tommy reflects on how the incident changed his perspective and shares his insights into human behavior.

These days, Tommy works in real estate, flipping old houses to reveal their full potential. He enjoys more than anything spending time with his son, Reece. They live in Austin, Texas.

~

Jessica Hagemann is an Austin-based ghostwriter. You may contact her at www.ciderspoonstories.com or ciderspoon@gmail.com.

www.ingramcontent.com/pod-product-compliance
Lightning Source LLC
Chambersburg PA
CBHW070824180526
45168CB00002B/737